MARK ZUCKERBERG:

FROM FACEBOOK TO FAMOUS

EXTRAORDINARY SUCCESS WITH A HIGH SCHOOL DIPLOMA OR LESS

JENNIFER ANISTON: FROM FRIENDS TO FILMS

TYRA BANKS: FROM THE RUNWAY TO THE TELEVISION SCREEN

HALLE BERRY: FROM BEAUTY QUEEN TO OSCAR WINNER

JAMES CAMERON: FROM TRUCK DRIVER TO DIRECTOR

SIMON COWELL: FROM THE MAILROOM TO IDOL FAME

ELLEN DEGENERES: FROM COMEDY CLUB TO TALK SHOW

MICHAEL DELL: FROM CHILD ENTREPRENEUR TO COMPUTER MAGNATE

STEVE JOBS: FROM APPLES TO APPS

RACHAEL RAY: FROM CANDY COUNTER TO COOKING SHOW

RUSSELL SIMMONS: FROM THE STREETS TO THE MUSIC BUSINESS

JIM SKINNER: FROM BURGERS TO THE BOARDROOM

HARRY TRUMAN: FROM FARMER TO PRESIDENT

MARK ZUCKERBERG: FROM FACEBOOK TO FAMOUS

MARK ZUCKERBERG:

FROM FACEBOOK TO FAMOUS

by Z. B. Hill

Mason Crest

MARK ZUCKERBERG: *FROM FACEBOOK TO FAMOUS*

Mason Crest
370 Reed Road
Broomall, Pennsylvania 19008
www.masoncrest.com

Printed and bound in the United States of America.

First printing
9 8 7 6 5 4 3 2 1

Library of Congress Cataloging-in-Publication Data

Hill, Z. B.
  Mark Zuckerberg : from Facebook to famous / Z.B. Hill.
     p. cm. — (Extraordinary success with a high school diploma or less)
  Includes index.
   ISBN 978-1-4222-2303-1 (hard cover) — ISBN 978-1-4222-2293-5 (series hardcover) — ISBN 978-1-4222-9365-2 (ebook)
 1. Zuckerberg, Mark, 1984- 2. Facebook (Firm) 3. Facebook (Electronic resource) 4. Webmasters—United States—Biography. 5. Computer software developers—United States—Biography. 6. Businesspeople—United States—Biography. 7. Online social networks. I. Title.
  HM479.Z83H55 2012
  006.7092—dc23
  [B]
                              2011023726

Produced by Harding House Publishing Services, Inc.
www.hardinghousepages.com
Interior design by Camden Flath.
Cover design by Torque Advertising + Design.

CONTENTS

INTRODUCTION

Finding a great job without a college degree is hard to do—but it's possible. In fact, more and more, going to college doesn't necessarily guarantee you a job. In the past few years, only one in four college graduates find jobs in their field. And, according to the U.S. Bureau of Labor Statistics, eight out of the ten fastest-growing jobs don't require college degrees.

But that doesn't mean these jobs are easy to get. You'll need to be willing to work hard. And you'll also need something else. The people who build a successful career without college are all passionate about their work. They're excited about it. They're committed to getting better and better at what they do. They don't just want to make money. They want to make money doing something they truly love.

So a good place for you to start is to make a list of the things you find really interesting. What excites you? What do you love doing? Is there any way you could turn that into a job?

Now talk to people who already have jobs in that field. How did they get where they are today? Did they go to college—or did they find success through some other route? Do they know anyone else you can talk to? Talk to as many people as you can to get as many perspectives as possible.

According to the U.S. Department of Labor, two out of every three jobs require on-the-job training rather than a college degree. So your next step might be to find an entry-level position in the field that interests you. Don't expect to start at the top. Be willing to learn while you work your way up from the bottom.

That's what almost all the individuals in this series of books did: they started out somewhere that probably seemed pretty distant from their end goal—but it was actually the first step in their journey. Celebrity Simon Cowell began his career working in a mailroom. Jim Skinner, who ended up running McDonald's Corporation, started out flipping burgers. World-famous cook Rachael Ray worked at a candy counter. All these people found incredible success without a college degree—but they all had a dream of where they wanted to go in life . . . and they were willing to work hard to make their dream real.

Ask yourself: Do I have a dream? Am I willing to work hard to make it come true? The answers to those questions are important!

CHAPTER 1
EARLY LIFE

Words to Know

CEO: CEO stands for chief executive officer. A company's CEO runs the company and makes important decisions about what the company will do or how it will work.

social networking: Social networking is people communicating and sharing information about themselves online.

psychiatrist: A psychiatrist is a kind of doctor who is an expert on diagnosing and treating mental illness.

computer programming: Computer programming involves creating instructions that tell a computer what to do. Computer programming can be used to create computer software like games or helpful programs used in business.

software: Computer software can describe any program that you use on your computer, whether a game or application used for work.

prodigy: A prodigy is someone who is very talented at something at a very early age.

In 2011, Mark Zuckerberg had a very special guest come to the offices of Facebook, the company Mark had started in his college dorm room just seven years earlier. Facebook had made Mark the youngest billionaire in the world. But at only twenty-seven years old, the **CEO** and president of Facebook wasn't known for acting like a regular businessman.

Mark liked working at Facebook's offices in a hooded sweatshirt, rather than in a suit like many other billionaire CEOs.

His guest introduced himself by saying, "My name is Barack Obama and I'm the guy who got Mark to wear a jacket and tie. I'm very proud of that."

Not every company gets a visit from the President of the United States, but Facebook is no ordinary company. The company's website helped change the way people communicate, how people use the Internet, and the way people share information about themselves online. In an age when the Internet is one of the main ways people get their information about the world around them, as well as how they communicate with their friends and family, Mark and his company Facebook have been a leading force in the movement toward a more connected world.

President Barack Obama noted that Facebook was part of this global change as he explained why he had decided to hold an event at the company's headquarters:

> The reason we want to do this is because more and more people are getting their information through different media. Historically, part of what makes for a healthy democracy, what makes good politics, is citizens who are informed and engaged. And Facebook allows us to make sure this isn't a one-way conversation.

Mark founded the ***social networking*** website Facebook.com in 2004, and by 2011, hundreds of millions of people used the site.

President Barack Obama visited Mark's company, Facebook, in 2011. At one point in the visit, Mark pointed out that he had no problem paying higher taxes.

Facebook's success and a movie based on his life helped Mark Zuckerberg become a household name.

And Mark's achieved all this without a college degree.

The College Choice

The fact that Mark Zuckerberg never graduated from college is surprising, considering the success he's achieved in technology and business. Today, for many high school graduates, going to college simply seems like the next step. More than 70 percent of high school students graduating in 2009 went on to college the next year. Going to college can be a path to a wide variety of jobs in many different fields. Without some type of college

Mark's parents raised their gifted son in the town of Dobbs Ferry, New York, where Mark's father ran a dental practice.

education, it's impossible to become a doctor, lawyer, professor, or scientist, for instance. But attending college is also a choice, and it's not for everyone.

Though many high school students don't give a second thought to applying to colleges in their senior year, some young adults achieve success without having a college degree. Entering the workforce right out of high school can be rewarding and exciting. College won't necessarily prepare you for every career, and many professionals learn what they need to know on the job. In addition, many high school students graduate knowing exactly what they want to do for a living, and it may not require attending a college. Many paths lead to success; college is often just one of them.

From an early age, Mark knew what he wanted to do with his life, and he took the time to teach himself the skills needed to pursue his goals. Mark has spent much of his life learning about the things that interest him, developing his passions outside of school. That drive to know more and to do the best he can has made Mark Zuckerberg the success he is today.

Early Life

Mark Zuckerberg was born on May 14, 1984, in the city of White Plains, New York. He grew up living with his family in Dobbs Ferry, New York. Mark's parents' names are Edward and Karen, and he has three sisters, Randi, Arielle, and Donna.

Mark's father, Edward, worked as a dentist in Dobbs Ferry, where his patients called him "painless Dr. Z" for the gentle way he treated them. Edward's dental office is attached to the house where Mark and his sisters grew up, allowing him to work close to his family. Mark's mother, Karen, worked as a **psychiatrist** for a time, but she left the field to care for Mark and his three sisters. She also worked in Edward's dental office, helping him to run and organize his business.

Edward's dental practice exposed him to early computer technology, particularly when it came to X-rays and organizing his office. That experience with technology rubbed off on Mark, helping to shape his interests early in his life. Edward introduced Mark to **computer programming.** He showed his son how to program using an Atari computer, an early, simple kind of home computer, much less powerful than the computers in our homes today. Mark learned quickly, and he soon found he had a real passion for computers and programming.

In 1996, Edward wished aloud for a way for his office receptionist to tell him that a patient had arrived in the waiting room. Up to that point, his receptionist had simply been yelling into the office, and Edward wanted something more efficient. Twelve-year-old Mark saw that a computer program could help solve his father's problem. He set to work to create **software** that could help.

The program that Mark built enabled the computers in his father's dental office and in the Zuckerberg house to send messages back and forth. Mark called his creation Zucknet. The program's name was a reference to Mark's nickname, "Zuck."

A year later, America Online (AOL) released its own messaging program, called Instant Messenger, but Mark had already seen the potential for computers to communicate with each other over the Internet. Zucknet allowed Edward's recep-

Early computers like this Atari 400 allowed young people interested in computers and programming to have their first hands-on experience.

tionist to send a message to him whenever a patient arrived. Using the program Mark created, Edward and his family could send messages between the computers in their home, as well. One night, Mark used Zucknet to send a message to his sister Donna while she did her homework. The message said that a computer virus would cause the computer she was on to explode in thirty seconds!

Continuing to Learn About Computers

Mark's parents, realizing that their son had a gift for computer programming, soon hired a tutor to teach Mark more about his passion. David Newman, a software programmer, began visiting the Zuckerberg home each week to teach Mark more about computer programming and creating software. When interviewed later in his life, Newman told New Yorker magazine that Mark was "a **prodigy**" when it came to programming. "It was tough to stay ahead of him," Newman said.

Mark started creating his own games, using his skills as a computer programmer. "I had a bunch of friends who were artists," he told a magazine interviewer. "They'd come over, draw stuff, and I'd build a game out of it." Mark loved to create new things through computer programming, whether games or new ways to communicate using computers.

When Mark was a little older, his parents helped him take a college computer class at Mercy College, a college near the Zuckerbergs' Dobbs Ferry home. Each Thursday night, Mark's father Edward would drive him to the school and drop Mark off to attend the class. The first time Mark's dad dropped him off at the class, the teacher told him he couldn't bring his son inside with him. Edward had to tell the professor that it was his son who'd be taking the class, not him.

A Bright Student

Mark started high school at a school called Ardsley High School, located in Ardsley, New York. While at Ardsley, Mark studied hard and got excellent grades. He was particularly interested in Greek and Latin studies. Mark loved to read classical literature and found he enjoyed taking classes on the languages in which works like *The Iliad* and *The Odyssey* were originally written. By

Mark's sophomore year, his family realized he needed more than what Ardsley High School could offer him, so Mark applied to a boarding school called Phillips Exeter Academy, called Exeter for short. Mark was accepted at Exeter, and he moved into the dorms at the Exeter, New Hampshire school.

At Exeter, Mark continued to do very well in school and in activities outside the classroom. He kept up his love of classical literature, Latin, and Greek. Mark also became an excellent fencer and became captain of Exeter's fencing team by the time he graduated from the school. In addition, he won prizes for his work in math, physics, and astronomy, as well as for his studies in Latin and Greek.

Mark graduated from Phillips Exeter Academy having already created a successful computer program. He was ready for the world of Harvard.

At the time Mark left high school, he was already primed for success in the information technology industry, but he was also ready to make his own way.

Though he was always able to succeed in the classroom, Mark's passion for computers never took a back seat to his other activities. While at Exeter, he continued to learn more about computer programming and create new software using his skills.

During his senior year, Mark created a computer program for his senior project called Synapse Media Player. Synapse was a program that recorded what kind of music users liked to hear, keeping track of the songs and artists they enjoyed. The program then automatically picked new artists, new songs, and new playlists for users based on the music they'd already listened to. You might know the website called Pandora.com that similarly picks music for users based on what they already like. At the time, however, Mark's Synapse Media Player was a new idea. What started as a senior project from a high school student quickly spread on the Internet. Blogs and websites wrote about Synapse, and Internet users began downloading the project for themselves. To put out Synapse, Mark started a company he called Intelligent Media Group.

Big Internet and technology companies started to take notice of Mark's program and the buzz that it was getting on the Internet. Soon, Microsoft and AOL were both trying to buy Synapse from Mark and offering him jobs creating software at their companies. Mark turned them both down and decided instead to go on to college after graduating from Exeter. Mark wasn't even eighteen yet, but he already showed great promise.

CHAPTER 2
CREATING FACEBOOK

Words to Know

prestigious: Prestigious means important and highly regarded.

fraternity: A fraternity is a social organization of male students on a college campus.

hacking: Hacking is using a computer to get around another computer's security.

undergraduate: Undergraduate students are college students who haven't gotten their degrees yet. Many universities have both undergraduate students and graduate students, who are trying to earn a second, higher-level degree.

inevitable: If something is inevitable, it is definitely going to happen; there's no avoiding it.

controversial: If something is controversial, it causes disagreement.

After graduating from Exeter, Mark decided to attend Harvard University, one of the best colleges in the country. When he applied to the *prestigious* school, Mark had plenty to put on his college application. He could speak and write French, Hebrew, Latin, and Greek. He'd won prizes for his work in many different subjects in school and been the captain of his school's fencing team. Mark had even created a computer program that resulted in job offers from two of the world's biggest companies, AOL and Microsoft. He was accepted to the school during his senior year at Exeter, and he began attending classes in the fall of 2002.

College Life

At Harvard, Mark began to take classes in psychology and computer science. He joined the university's Jewish *fraternity*, Alpha Epsilon Pi. At a party at the fraternity's house one Friday night, Mark met Priscilla Chan, whom Mark has dated ever since. Between classes and fraternity activities, Mark continued to create computer software, and he also started building websites.

During his second year at Harvard, Mark created a program called CourseMatch, which allowed users to decide on which classes to take based on other people in the class. He also created a website called Facemash, a very simple site that allowed users to see photos of two people and then vote on who was better looking. The site used photos of students at Harvard, which Mark got by *hacking* Harvard's computer network, taking pictures of students. In its first few hours online, a few hundred people visited Facemash.

Over the next few days the site was shared with people around Harvard, leading the school's administration to take notice and shut down the site. The administration was furious that Mark had gotten through the security surrounding their network and taken images of students. They threatened to kick him out of school, but eventually, they decided to let him stay at the university.

After Facemash was shut down, articles about Mark appeared in the Harvard student newspaper, and students were both outraged at and interested in their fellow classmate. Soon, three students looking to start their own site came to Mark for help. Divya Narendra and Cameron and Tyler Winklevoss wanted to create a website that allowed students at Harvard to find each other online, share information, and possibly begin dating. They called the site Harvard Connection. Mark agreed to help Narendra and the Winklevoss brothers (two twins known to other students for their spots on Harvard's rowing team) in the creation of Harvard Connection.

Divya Narendra and Cameron and Tyler Winklevoss maintain that they created the idea for Facebook with their site Harvard Connection.

Cameron Winklevoss and his brother Tyler both rowed for the United States in the 2008 Olympics in Beijing, China. Both rowed at Harvard as well.

Starting Facebook

Mark worked with Narendra and the Winklevoss twins on Harvard Connection, but it wasn't long before he stopped working on the site. Instead, he began work on his own web project, a site that allowed users to post information about themselves and see information posted by other students. He called his site TheFacebook.com, based, many believe, on the books Exeter gave students that included pictures, addresses, and phone numbers for every student in the school. "Face books" were a way for students to get to know each other at a new school, and Mark thought a similar idea could work online. Mark wanted the site to be easy to use and reasonably simple, so that anyone could use it. He made the main color on the site blue, because of his colorblindness; he can't see red or green. Blue was the color Mark could see most clearly, making the decision to go with blue and white an easy one. "Blue is the richest color for me," he later told an interviewer. "I can see all of blue."

In his sophomore year at Harvard, Mark launched TheFacebook.com as a way for students at the university to share information. The reaction from students on campus was very positive, and the site became quite popular. Students began sharing information about themselves, creating profiles and pages that explained their interests and contained their photos. Within one month of the site's launch on February 4, 2004, almost half of Harvard **undergraduate** students had signed up for TheFacebook.com and created their own pages on the site.

After the successful launch of TheFacebook.com, Mark worked with his friends at Harvard, Eduardo Savarin, Chris Hughes, and Dustin Moskovitz, to develop more ideas for the site. The friends had long talked about how the Internet would become more and more popular, until everyone used it. Looking back on his creating TheFacebook.com, Mark told an interviewer about his discussions with his friends:

> [We] would hang out and go together to Pinocchio's, the local pizza place, and talk about trends in technology. We'd say, "Isn't it obvious that everyone was going to be on the Internet? Isn't it, like, *inevitable* that there would be a huge social network of people?" It was something that we expected to happen. The thing that's been really surprising about the evolution of Facebook is—I think then and I think now—that if we didn't do this someone else would have done it.

Though the site began as Harvard-only, Facebook soon expanded to other top-level universities, particularly with the help of Mark's friends Dustin Moskovitz and Chris Hughes. TheFacebook.com started to allow students from Boston University, New York University, Columbia, Yale, Dartmouth, and Stanford to create their own profiles. Soon, the site became open to students from colleges all over United States.

By the end of his second year at Harvard, Mark was ready to drop out of college and run Facebook full-time. Soon, the

Though Facebook's start was controversial, today, the company—and Mark—have become incredibly successful.

company would become one of the Internet's most successful, its website used by millions all over the world. But Mark's rise to success with Facebook wasn't without a difficult start.

Controversial Beginnings

Despite the early success of Mark's Facebook.com, the site's beginnings remain *controversial*. The students who worked with Mark for a little while on Harvard Connection believe that Mark stole the idea for Facebook from them. "[Mark] stole the moment, he stole the idea, and he stole the execution," Cameron Winklevoss told an interviewer years later. A few days after Mark launched TheFacebook.com at Harvard, Divya Narendra

Not long after Mark created Facebook, he left Harvard and was on his way to the next phase of his life, as the head of a major company.

and the Winklevoss twins, Cameron and Tyler, told the student newspaper that Mark had told them he was helping to build Harvard Connection while working on his own site based on the same idea. They said Mark had lied to them about working on Harvard Connection and ended up taking their idea, leaving them with nothing.

Mark sees things very differently. He says that Harvard Connection focused on dating, while his site was based around the idea of sharing information. Mark has said that he created Facebook without inspiration from the Harvard Connection project, despite the close timing of his working on Harvard Connection and starting Facebook.

Regardless of how Mark got the idea for TheFacebook.com, when the site launched, it quickly became a huge success. Though it started small its reach grew quickly, and soon college students from all over the country were creating Facebook pages for themselves. With Mark leaving college, he'd have the time to focus on growing the site even more and creating what would become one of the Internet's biggest success stories.

CHAPTER 3
THE SOCIAL NETWORK

Words to Know

investors: Investors give money to companies in exchange for part of the money that company makes later.

incorporated: When a company becomes incorporated, it has the legal rights of a human being.

applications: Applications are programs or groups of programs designed for end users.

lawsuit: A lawsuit is a disagreement between two people or groups brought to a court to be decided or settled.

nominated: To be nominated means to be selected as one of a small group up for an award.

portrayed: If someone is portrayed, he is shown in some way through art, literature, a movie, or a play.

After the launch of Facebook in early 2004, Mark left college to focus on building the site and creating a company to help manage it. He was certain he didn't need a college education to achieve his goals.

To grow the new company, Mark moved to California, met **investors**, and opened up Facebook to new users. Over the next few years, Facebook would become one of the most important new Internet companies in the world, and the site's popularity would grow each year. New ideas and new users kept Facebook fresh and interesting, attracting even more people to the top social networking site.

Before the success, however, the company's first year began in a small house in California.

Moving Facebook to California

In the summer of 2004, with TheFacebook.com growing in popularity, Facebook **incorporated**. Sean Parker, the creator of the Internet music-sharing program Napster, had been giving advice to Mark about how to grow Facebook and start a company. When Facebook officially became a company, Sean became its president.

In June of the same year, Mark moved to Palo Alto, California, with a few of the friends who'd helped him start TheFacebook.com, including Dustin Moskovitz. The group rented a small house that served as the Facebook offices, as well as the home for the people who worked at the small company.

To start a new company is very difficult, but without money to pay for things like offices, computers, and the salaries of people who work at the company, it's nearly impossible. To keep Facebook going, Mark needed to find an investor who was willing to provide the company with some of the money he'd need to run the business. In the summer that Facebook moved to California, Mark, Dustin Moskovitz, and Chris Hughes met with a business-

Peter Thiel, the man behind internet company PayPal and others, was just the person Mark needed to help take Facebook to the next level.

man named Peter Thiel. Peter is best known for helping to start PayPal, a system that allows Internet users to pay for the things they buy online using a credit card. With PayPal, Internet sites big and small can use a system that's already been created, rather than having to build their own, which would cost them time and money. PayPal had become a success with the increase in the number of Internet users shopping online, and Peter had started working to find companies in which to invest. Facebook was just the right kind of company for Peter's investment. At the meeting with Mark, Dustin, and Chris, Peter agreed to give half a billion dollars to the new company.

Now Facebook had the money it needed to continue to grow, and its founders were ready to work hard to make that happen. Mark and his friends had big plans for Facebook. Moving to California was just the beginning!

Palo Alto and Silicon Valley

Palo Alto is home to many of the largest and most important technology companies in the United States. Stanford University, one of the best universities in the country, is also there, as well as computer company Hewlett-Packard and electric car company Tesla Motors. Google, PayPal, Logitech, and Sun Microsystems have all been located in Palo Alto, particularly early in their history.

Palo Alto is considered part of what is called Silicon Valley, an area of California near San Francisco in which many of the country's technology companies are based or have started. Silicon Valley is often thought of as the center of the technology, Internet, and computer industries in the United States and even the world.

The name "Silicon Valley" was first used in 1971, when the name appeared in a magazine article called "Silicon Valley in the USA." The "valley" is the Santa Clara Valley near San Francisco. Silicon is a material used in computer parts. Apple, Intel, Twitter, EBay, Yahoo!, and many other technology companies have been based in Silicon Valley at some point, and some of the biggest companies in the world were founded in the area.

Facebook Grows

In 2005, Facebook bought the right to use the name Facebook.com and changed the name of their site, losing "The" from the beginning of the site's name. In the same year, Facebook opened their site to high school students who wanted to sign up and create their own pages. Before that point, Facebook had only been open to college students. Then, the company allowed the employees of a few important technology companies like Apple and Microsoft to join the site and begin sharing information about themselves. About a year later, in September of 2006, Facebook opened the site to anyone older than thirteen who had an e-mail address. From there, the company began to grow rapidly.

A huge number of successful technology companies are based in the Silicon Valley, including Mark's company Facebook.

Just two years later, in August of 2008, Facebook.com had 100 million users. Mark took note of the achievement in a blog post on the site:

> We hit a big milestone today—100 million people around the world are now using Facebook. This is a really gratifying moment for us because it means a lot that you have decided that Facebook is a good, trusted place for you to share your lives with your friends. So we just wanted to take this moment to say, "thanks."

Facebook's Silicon Valley offices have come a long way from the California house Mark and his Facebook coworkers lived in when Facebook first started.

We spend all our time here trying to build the best possible product that enables you to share and stay connected, so the fact that we're growing so quickly all over the world is very rewarding. Thanks for all your support and stay tuned for more great things in the future.

One hundred million users might seem like a lot—and it is!—but that was just the start of Facebook's extraordinary growth. Only six months later, Mark posted on Facebook.com again announcing that the site had reached 200 million people using the site. By early 2010, 400 million people had signed up for the site to share information and connect with their friends. A few months after that, in the summer of 2010, Facebook.com had half a billion people using the site.

Along with new users, came more money for Facebook. In 2006, the company made just over $50 million, a lot for a new company, but very little compared to how much Facebook would go on to make. In 2007, for instance, the company made three times what it did the year before. By 2009, Facebook made three quarters of a billion dollars, and just one year later, the company brought in around $2 billion.

In just a few years, Facebook had gone from its beginnings in a college dorm room to becoming one of the biggest companies on the Internet. Mark's dream of creating a social networking site that allowed people from all over the world to share information about themselves with their friends and family had come true. He'd once made games and small programs in his parents' house.

Today, Facebook continues to grow and expand its reach. Facebook is one of Silicon Valley's most successful companies.

By 2010, he was running a company that many considered to be one of the most important of the Internet age. And he'd done all that without a college degree.

New Features and New Ideas

Facebook has changed a lot since it first began. Changes have helped bring new people onto Facebook and keep users who have been on the site for years interested in continuing to log on. One of the biggest and most important new ideas from Facebook has been Facebook Platform, which has helped spread Facebook's influence around the Internet and brought new features to the site itself.

Facebook Platform is a way for other companies and designers to use tools created by Facebook to change and add to the website. Using Facebook Platform, other companies can take advantage of the things that Facebook does to make what they do better or create entirely new uses for the social networking website. With the Platform, companies have created games that can be played by users and added other new ideas to Facebook, allowing users to do new things on the site.

By 2010, more than half a million *applications* had been created by companies and people around the world. These applications have also created new business opportunities for many companies. Zynga, a company that makes games for Facebook such as Farmville, has made hundreds of millions of dollars through their use of the Facebook Platform.

Facebook Platform also allows other websites to bring Facebook to their site. Users can now use Facebook features while reading their favorite blog or watching videos online on a different website. They can "Like" an article and have it show up on their Facebook profile. Users can see which of their friends have read the same article and see which other articles and websites they've shared. Facebook is now connected to sites all over the Internet, helping to make it one of the major ways people share information online. The site itself is also much more than sharing information or pictures, thanks to Facebook Platform bringing games and other features to the biggest social networking site on the Internet.

Controversy Over Facebook's Founding Continues

In 2004, after Facebook had launched and become a success, Divya Narendra and the Winklevoss twins, Cameron and Tyler, filed a *lawsuit* against Facebook, accusing Mark and the company of taking their idea for a social networking site that would connect Harvard students. The group of Harvard graduates, who had changed their site's name from Harvard Connection to ConnectU, said they deserved some of the money Facebook was making.

The lawsuit took four years to come to an end, and in that time, Facebook had become a giant of the Internet business world. To end the lawsuit against them, the social networking company ended up paying the founders of ConnectU $65 million in 2008. The $65 million was an amount based on how much Facebook was worth at that time, but not long after Facebook paid ConnectU the money, Divya Narendra and the Winklevoss twins said that Facebook had lied about how much it was actually worth, and they wanted more money from the company. In 2009, a judge rejected that second lawsuit, deciding that Facebook was telling the truth and that Mark's company hadn't tricked the founders of ConnectU into taking less than they deserved.

The controversy over Facebook's beginnings was finally finished for Mark and his company. They'd paid the founders of ConnectU to drop their lawsuit, and that brought about an end to stories in newspapers and online that questioned whether Mark was honest about his company's start. But in 2010, the story about Facebook's founding would be told again, and in a way that it hadn't before.

Mark's Life on the Big Screen

In October of 2010, Columbia Pictures released a movie based on the first few years of Facebook called *The Social Network*. *The Social Network* tells the story of how Mark started Facebook at Harvard and turned the website into a successful company, while also focusing on the controversy surrounding the website's start and the legal battles Mark faced in the years after Facebook was founded.

David Fincher directed the movie, which was written by Aaron Sorkin and starred actor Jesse Eisenberg as Mark Zuckerberg. Justin Timberlake, Andrew Garfield, and Rashida Jones also star in the movie. The director, David Fincher, is best known for his movies *Seven*, *The Game*, *Fight Club*, and *The Curious Case of Benjamin Button*. Writer Aaron Sorkin is best known for his work on the television show *The West Wing* and the movie *A Few Good Men*, based on a play of the same name Sorkin had written earlier. Nine Inch Nails singer Trent Reznor and musician Atticus Ross created the music for the movie.

The Social Network became a huge hit. The movie made more than $200 million around the world and was **nominated** for many awards, including Golden Globes and Oscars. In early 2011, The Social Network won more Golden Globes than any other film from 2010, including awards for Best Screenplay for Aaron Sorkin and Best Director for David Fincher. The movie also won Best Motion Picture—Drama, an award that many consider the most important of the Golden Globes. At the 2011 Oscars, *The Social Network* was nominated for Best Picture, Best Director, and Best Actor, among others, but ended up winning Best Adapted Screenplay, Best Original Score, and Best Film Editing. Critics loved the movie, and some said it was the best of the last ten years.

The movie didn't paint the most flattering picture of Mark. In the film, he is **portrayed** as being somewhat dishonest, possibly taking the idea for Facebook from the creators of Harvard Connection, the Winklevoss twins and Divya Narendra. The Mark in the movie betrays the friends that help him start Facebook, eventually kicking them out of the company.

Mark wasn't thrilled that a movie about his life made him out to be a disloyal friend looking to make as much money for himself as possible. "I just wished that nobody made a movie of me while I was still alive," Mark told a reporter.

The Social Network writer Aaron Sorkin based his script on a book by author Ben Mezrich called *The Accidental Billionaires*. The book told the story of Facebook's founding, but some critics say that the book is more fiction than fact. Mezrich didn't talk to Mark Zuckerberg while writing the book, but he did talk to Eduardo Saverin, one of the friends who helped Mark start the site. Eduardo was in the middle of a lawsuit against Mark during the writing of the book, but once that was settled, he stopped talking to Mezrich. After *The Social Network* came out, many of the people portrayed in the movie spoke up to say that the movie was a good story but not really based on what actually happened in the first few years of Facebook. "A lot of exciting things happened in 2004, but mostly we just worked a lot and stressed out about things," Dustin Moskovitz said. "It's just cool to see a dramatization of history." Writer Aaron Sorkin said that he cared more about making the story interesting than making it completely true.

Whether or not *The Social Network* gave an accurate picture of Mark and the founding of Facebook, it certainly helped make Mark more famous than he already was. In addition, the movie was a clear sign that Facebook had become a massive success. How many websites can boast that they have a movie based on their start? Mark and his website had become famous!

CHAPTER 4
MARK TODAY

Words to Know

philanthropy: Philanthropy is charity, giving money to others for the purpose of making people's lives better.

foundation: A foundation is an organization that is often non-profit; in other words, it receives no money for the work it does.

anonymously: If you do something anonymously, you do it without letting others know it was you.

conflated: If two things are conflated, they get combined or mixed up with each other.

detractors: Detractors are people who criticize someone or something.

passive: If someone is passive, she receives information or actions without responding to it in any active way.

icons: Icons are people or things regarded as being symbols of something bigger.

Mark Zuckerberg has become famous for the success he's had with Facebook and the movie based on his life. Today, he's also working hard to share his success with others and use his fame to inspire charity and giving on the part of some of the wealthiest people in the world. Despite all of his success and fame, however, Mark still runs Facebook, is still dating his long-time girlfriend Priscilla Chan, still drives a modest car, and still wears hooded sweatshirts and t-shirts to work.

Giving Back

The year 2010 was an important one for Mark. Not only did his life become a major movie, he also began putting a lot of the money he'd made through Facebook toward *philanthropy*. Mark understood that his success could be used to help others, and that by making more money than most people, he had to make sure his money did more than sit in a bank account. By helping others, Mark was putting his success to good use.

In September of 2010, Mark announced that he would be starting a new *foundation* called Start Up: Education. The foundation's goal would be to improve the state of the nation's education system, with its first project being to work with the government of New Jersey to improve Newark, New Jersey's school system. Mark donated $100 million dollars to the project, hoping he could help make Newark's schools an example to the entire country. Mark worked with Governor Chris Christie and Newark Mayor Corey Booker to try to raise more money to match the $100 million he was giving, all in the name of improving education for kids. Mark wanted them to have the same shot at a great education that he did.

At first, because of the timing of his donation just before the release of *The Social Network*, Mark wanted to give the money to help Newark's schools *anonymously*. Some people thought Mark wanted to give the money to make himself look better before the

Actor Jesse Eisenberg played Mark in The Social Network, *increasing his own fame as well as the Facebook founder's.*

movie came out. They said he was trying to donate the money to get ahead of negative responses to the version of himself shown in *The Social Network*. "The thing that I was most sensitive about with the movie timing was, I didn't want the press about *The Social Network* movie to get **conflated** with the Newark project," Mark told reporters at the time. "I was thinking about doing this anonymously just so that the two things could be kept separate." Mark had to be convinced by Governor Christie and Mayor Booker to give the money publicly, without keeping his name out of things.

In addition to the money he put up to help the schools in Newark, Mark also announced in 2010 that he had signed the Giving Pledge, an agreement between some of the world's wealthiest people to give away at least half their money to charity over time. Billionaires Bill Gates and Warren Buffet started the Giving Pledge as a way to encourage the wealthy to give more of their money to charity, and Mark was eager to sign on.

Famous for Facebook

Thanks to Facebook and *The Social Network*, Mark has become one of business's biggest names. His fame comes from the fact that he's still young, that he's become very wealthy, and that his site is one of the most popular on the Internet. In 2010, Mark seemed to be everywhere. Whether it was interviews about Facebook or buzz about the movie based on his life, Mark's life and work was a major topic of conversation.

Mark was featured as a cartoon character on The Simpsons, *a hallmark of being truly famous.*

Mark played a cartoon version of himself on *The Simpsons*, lending his voice to an episode of the long-running show. In an episode called "Loan-a Lisa," the cartoon Mark Zuckerberg tells Lisa Simpson that she doesn't need to go to college to be successful in life. He tells her that he, Bill Gates, and Richard Branson all achieved their goals without the help of a college education and degree.

Mark visited *Saturday Night Live* when actor Jesse Eisenberg hosted the comedy show. On the show, Mark met Jesse for the first time. The two exchanged an awkward moment of silence while the audience laughed, before Jesse asked Mark if he'd seen *The Social Network*. Mark, dressed in his hooded sweatshirt, told Jesse that he did see the movie and that he thought it was "interesting," while flashing a big grin.

The Facebook founder visited Oprah Winfrey's show in 2010 to discuss his $100 million donation to the school system of Newark, New Jersey. New Jersey Governor Chris Christie and Newark Mayor Corey Booker went on the show with Mark to discuss how they would turn around Newark's education system. Mark had been on *Oprah* once before, but this time he was coming to the show as one of the most successful business people in the world offering a helping hand to a struggling city.

In 2011, President Barack Obama, one of the most recognizable people in the world, visited the Facebook offices to talk to the company's employees about politics in a question-and-answer meeting. The President answered questions from Mark and the staff at Facebook. The meeting was a sign of just how famous Mark and Facebook had become. When the President of the United States, a man known all over the world, not only knows your name but pays you a visit, you know you've made it!

Continuing Controversy

Although Facebook has become one of the most successful Internet companies, many question whether its impact has been positive or negative. Some wonder whether Facebook.com has changed the way people communicate with each other in a way that makes relationships less meaningful. Others question Facebook's treatment of the privacy of its users.

In 2010, when asked whether he sees Facebook as changing the definition of friendship for a new generation, making relationships between friends less meaningful, Mark said he doesn't think the company has done that. Mark believes Facebook has helped people become closer, no matter how far they may be from each other geographically. "[Facebook has] always had the goal of helping people connect with all the people that they want," Mark told *Time* magazine. Mark continued:

> Our mission hasn't been to make it so people connect with people that they didn't know. . . . It's just all about, you know, maybe you're not in the same place as your family or your friends right now, but you want to stay connected. I think Facebook gives people a tool to do that better, in ways they couldn't before. . . . What I think Facebook allows is for people to stay connected who aren't seeing each other in person everyday. . . . I don't think Facebook is taking away from any

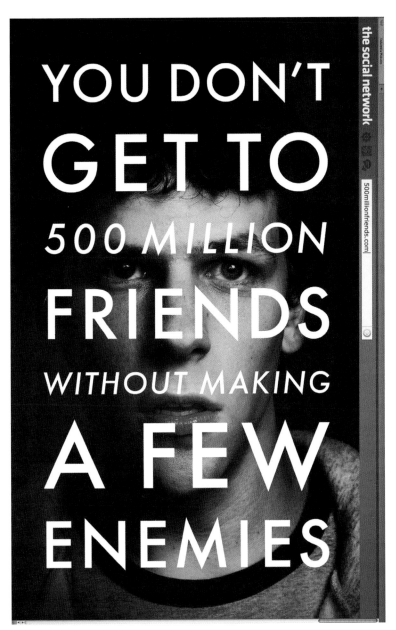

The poster from The Social Network *simply showed Jesse Eisenberg as Mark, in a photo similar to a Facebook profile image.*

of the other interactions that you have, it's just expanding your social sphere so that you can keep in touch with all of these people. Before, you just wouldn't have had any way to do that. That makes people's lives just a bit richer.

When discussing privacy with *Time* magazine, Mark said that he understands that people's privacy online is very important to them. He believes in users' ability to control what information is shared and with whom it's shared, but he also thinks that sharing photos or information about yourself with friends and family can be rewarding and important to bonding with others online. Mark has said that openly sharing information is an important part of Facebook's mission, that making the world a more open and less secretive place is part of a change that the Internet—and social networking companies like Facebook—is helping to bring about.

Critics, however, argue that Facebook doesn't allow users enough control over their privacy. They maintain that Facebook.com doesn't give users the options they would need to keep some information from being shared with others online, or even with big companies looking to advertise their products to Facebook's users. These critics also say that Facebook's privacy options are too difficult to use or understand, and that these options change too often for the average person to keep up with them.

Though Facebook may have its **detractors**, and debates over privacy and online relationships will continue, there's no questioning the massive change that Facebook and other social networking sites like it have helped bring to the world!

Success at a Young Age

Facebook is now used by hundreds of millions of people around the world. It has become one of the most successful websites on the Internet today. The site has changed the way people view and use the Internet, transforming the web from something that ordinary people couldn't change to something personal. No matter who you are, you can have a page on Facebook that allows you to speak your mind, share photos of yourself and your friends, and tell others what you're reading or watching online. What was once a *passive* experience for Internet users is now something in which each person can participate.

Facebook has helped people communicate ideas that have changed the future of countries around the world. Protests in Egypt, Iran, Syria, and other countries were helped by Facebook allowing people to communicate ideas that governments didn't allow their citizens to voice in newspapers or on the street. Some people have even called these movements "Facebook revolutions."

In 2010, almost one-quarter of the time that people used the Internet was on social networking sites like Facebook. Considering that e-mail accounted for only about 8 percent of all the time people spent online, that's a lot of time on Facebook and other sites like it! Facebook was also the site that, on average, people spent the most time on per month. On average, Internet users spent around two hours per month on Google.com and Yahoo.com, around half an hour on Amazon.com, but more than seven hours per month on Facebook.com.

With Facebook, Mark also helped create a new language of Facebook-related words. When someone says, "I have to update my status because my friend just poked me after I wrote on his wall," she is speaking in the language of Facebook, a language that didn't exist just a few years ago. Facebook has become part of our culture in a way that few businesses and websites have. Mark Zuckerberg has helped make it all possible—and he become famous himself in the process.

Mark's creation has helped change the way we use the Internet; it's changed the way we think about ideas of privacy and sharing online. What started as a project in his dorm room at Harvard University has now become on of the world's most important and well-known companies, rivaling other Internet giants like Google.

By 2011, at just twenty-seven years old, Mark had achieved more than most people will in their whole lives. He had become the youngest billionaire in the world. He'd been named by *Time* magazine as Person of the Year in 2010, an honor often reserved for political figures or world leaders. Mark joins popes and presidents, royalty and cultural **icons**, on the list of people who've been named Person of the Year by *Time*.

The cover of *Time*'s Person of the Year issue in 2010 simply showed a picture of Mark's face staring into the camera. The cover read, "Facebook's Mark Zuckerberg: The Connector." For the cover photo, most likely the most important of his entire life, one that millions around the world would see, Mark wore a t-shirt. Despite being the youngest billionaire on Earth, Mark certainly doesn't always act like he's the founder and CEO of one of the world's most important companies!

Mark Zuckerberg went from programming software in his bedroom at home to being one of the biggest names of the Internet age. He changed the world with Facebook. And he did it all without a college degree!

WHAT CAN YOU EXPECT?

Of course not everyone who skips college is going to be a celebrity or a millionaire. But there are other more ordinary jobs out there for people who choose to go a different route from college. Here's what you can expect to make in 100 of the top-paying jobs available to someone who has only a high school diploma. (If you're not sure what any of the jobs are, look them up on the Internet to find out more about them.) Keep in mind that these are average salaries; a beginning worker will likely make much less, while someone with many more years of experience could make much more. Also, remember that wages for the same jobs vary somewhat in different parts of the country.

Position	Average Annual Salary
rotary drill operators (oil & gas)	$59,560
commercial divers	$58,060
railroad conductors & yardmasters	$54,900
chemical plant & system operators	$54,010
real estate sales agents	$53,100
subway & streetcar operators	$52,800
postal service clerks	$51,670
pile-driver operators	$51,410
railroad brake, signal & switch operators	$49,600

brickmasons & blockmasons	$49,250
postal service mail carriers	$48,940
gaming supervisors	$48,920
postal service mail sorters & processors	$48,260
gas compressor & gas pumping station operators	$47,860
roof bolters (mining)	$47,750
forest fire fighters	$47,270
private detectives & investigators	$47,130
tapers	$46,880
continuous mining machine operators	$46,680
rail car repairers	$46,430
shuttle car operators	$46,400
rail-track laying & maintenance equipment operators	$46,000
chemical equipment operators & tenders	$45,100
explosives workers (ordnance handling experts & blasters)	$45,030
makeup artists (theatrical & performance)	$45,010
sheet metal workers	$44,890
managers/supervisors of landscaping & groundskeeping workers	$44,080
loading machine operators (underground mining)	$43,970
rough carpenters	$43,640

derrick operators (oil & gas)	$43,590
flight attendants	$43,350
refractory materials repairers (except brickmasons)	$43,310
production, planning & expediting clerks	$43,260
mine cutting & channeling machine operators	$43,120
fabric & apparel patternmakers	$42,940
service unit operators (oil, gas, & mining)	$42,690
tile & marble setters	$42,450
paperhangers	$42,310
bridge & lock tenders	$41,630
hoist & winch operators	$41,620
carpet installers	$41,560
pump operators (except wellhead pumpers)	$41,490
terrazzo workers & finishers	$41,360
plasterers & stucco masons	$41,260
painters (transportation equipment)	$41,220
automotive body & related repairers	$41,020
hazardous materials removal workers	$40,270
bailiffs	$40,240
wellhead pumpers	$40,210
maintenance workers (machinery)	$39,570
truck drivers (heavy & tractor-trailer)	$39,260

floor layers (except carpet, wood & hard tiles)	$39,190
managers of retail sales workers	$39,130
cargo & freight agents	$38,940
metal-refining furnace operators & tenders	$38,830
excavating & loading machine and dragline operators	$38,540
separating, filtering, clarifying & still machine operators	$38,450
motorboat operators	$38,390
dredge operators	$38,330
lay-out workers (metal & plastic)	$38,240
forest fire inspectors & prevention specialists	$38,180
medical & clinical laboratory technicians	$37,860
tire builders	$37,830
dental laboratory technicians	$37,690
paving, surfacing & tamping equipment operators	$37,660
locksmiths & safe repairers	$37,550
sailors & marine oilers	$37,310
dispatchers (except police, fire & ambulance)	$37,310
pipelayers	$37,040
helpers (extraction workers)	$36,870

rolling machine setters, operators & tenders	$36,670
welders, cutters & welder fitters	$36,630
solderers & brazers	$36,630
gem & diamond workers	$36,620
police, fire & ambulance dispatchers	$36,470
models	$36,420
meter readers (utilities)	$36,400
mechanical door repairers	$36,270
public address system & other announcers	$36,130
rail yard engineers, dinkey operators & hostlers	$36,090
bus drivers (transit & intercity)	$35,990
insurance policy processing clerks	$35,740
insurance claims clerks	$35,740
computer-controlled machine tool operators (metal and plastic)	$35,570
license clerks	$35,570
court clerks	$35,570
fallers	$35,570
septic tank servicers & sewer pipe cleaners	$35,470
parking enforcement workers	$35,360
highway maintenance workers	$35,310
floor sanders & finishers	$35,140

tool grinders, filers, & sharpeners	$35,110
paper goods machine setters, operators & tenders	$35,040
printing machine operators	$35,030
inspectors, testers, sorters, samplers & weighers	$34,840
pourers & casters (metal)	$34,760
loan interviewers & clerks	$34,670
furnace, kiln, oven, drier & kettle operators & tenders	$34,410
recreational vehicle service technicians	$34,320
roustabouts (oil & gas)	$34,190

Source: Bureau of Labor Statistics, U.S. Department of Labor, 2008.

Find Out More

In Books

Kirkpatrick, David. *The Facebook Effect: The Inside Story of the Company That Is Connecting the World.* New York: Simon & Schuster, 2011.

Mezrich, Ben. *The Accidental Billionaires: The Founding of Facebook: A Tale of Sex, Money, Genius and Betrayal.* New York: Doubleday, 2009.

Stewart, Gail B. *Mark Zuckerberg: Facebook Creator.* Farmington Hills, Minn.: Kid Haven, 2009.

On the Internet

Mark Zuckerberg's Page on Facebook
www.facebook.com/markzuckerberg

The New Yorker - The Face of Facebook: Mark Zuckerberg Opens Up
www.newyorker.com/reporting/2010/09/20/100920fa_fact_vargas

Time Magazine: Person of the Year 2010—Mark Zuckerberg
www.time.com/time/specials/packages/article/0,28804,2036683_2037183_2037185,00.html

Index

Picture Credits

Columbia Pictures: pp. 47, 51
Facebook: pp. 8, 27, 28, 36, 38, 44
Fox: p. 48
Henderson, Jim: p. 12
Krupa, Charles: p. 23
Mad Magazine: p. 22
McCormick: p. 15
Nagel, Bart: p. 33
Roee, Johnny: p. 24
Saujnier, Jared: p. 17
Solis, Brian: p. 18
The White House: p. 11

To the best knowledge of the publisher, all images not specifically credited are in the public domain. If any image has been inadvertently uncredited, please notify Harding House Publishing Services, 220 Front Street, Vestal, New York 13850, so that credit can be given in future printings.

About the Author

Z.B. Hill is a an author and publicist living in Binghamton, New York. He has written a number of books for young adults.